CHURCH
Is Not
ENOUGH

LATISHA COOPER JAMES

Book Cover Design: Prize Publishing House

Printed by Prize Publishing House, LLC in the United States of America.

First printing edition 2025.

Prize Publishing House
P.O. Box 9856, Chesapeake, VA 23321
www.PrizePublishingHouse.com

ISBN (Paperback): 979-8-9925617-8-4
ISBN (E-Book): 979-8-9925617-9-1

Library of Congress Control Number: 2025910400

Contents

Introduction

Many of us were raised in the church. We attended church regularly. Church was imposed on us. Parents quoted, "As for me and my house, we shall serve the Lord," often, especially when anyone in the house showed any sign of being uninterested in this "church stuff." Unfortunately, this was the stance, but there was not enough teaching or demonstration of what serving God looks like beyond simply attending church. Children did not receive sufficient guidance to cultivate their hearts to desire to serve God. Consequently, as many grew older, they drifted away. This drift from God mainly stemmed from our lack of knowing Him on a personal level or having a true relationship with Him.

I believe that when children have strong relationships and connections with God, they won't want to leave Him. If something happens that leads them to decide to walk away from God, it will be a difficult choice, but they will possess the "tools" and understanding needed to return to God swiftly.

As we learn and understand more every day, our parents raised us the best they "knew" how. Explaining and talking about "adult" things with children was just not something previous generations did. It was "do what I say, not what I do." You definitely couldn't ask questions for clarity or understanding; that was considered straight disrespect.

But let's set the record straight. I do not want to move any further without clearing this up. I feel I need to take this time to express this. Church is important! Going to church regularly is extremely beneficial for saints and ain'ts. My position in this book doesn't negate this belief at all. I'm simply suggesting that going to church alone is just not enough. It is not enough for adults, and it is definitely not enough for children. It is going to take more than attending church services to truly get to know God on a level that allows you to live freely and abundantly. Now more than ever, it is crucial for everyone, especially our children, to know and love God deeply. There is so much going on in the world that has a direct effect on children and their futures, not just adults. We are facing violence at an all-time high. There is so much negativity on social media. Our economy shows no signs of getting better. The education and school systems are in great despair. Illnesses and sicknesses are leaving children as orphans way too soon. Children are struggling with anxiety and fear of the unknown more now than any other generation. There are just so many things happening in the world that make absolutely no sense and have invoked so much fear in people. We all need Jesus, even our children! Only He can provide the reassurance and hope that everything is going to be okay.

Similarly, we can't expect schools to teach our children everything they need to know; we can't expect the church to teach them all there is to learn about God and how to build that relationship. It's our responsibility as parents to help them understand and apply the word to situations in their own lives at every stage of their development. We can't expect children to discover who God is on their own when we only show them how they will need Him as adults. The truth is, they need Him NOW. They need Him as a child in their own way. They need Him in the issues they face as children, so they can apply those same characteristics of God as they grow and confront more serious situations. Allow your children to learn and understand God continually, based on experiences at each stage of their lives. Be sure to start that learning experience of God and who He is as early as possible, so they have a long list of reminders they can fully comprehend and remember, no matter how small or large.

Chapter One
IT'S TRADITION

"Thus, you nullify the word of God by your tradition that you have handed down. And you do many things like that."

—MARK 7:13, NIV

As a little girl, the memory of getting dressed up in big, fluffy dresses with lace socks and shiny dress shoes is surely embedded in many women's minds. Those ponytails adorned with bows and barrettes that matched those dresses can hardly be forgotten. Wearing those freshly ironed, perfectly creased pants with a white collared dress shirt buttoned all the way up, feeling nearly choked by it, was unforgettable for every little boy forced to look his Sunday best. How could any man not recall the bold, patterned clip-on ties they were compelled to wear and then happily rip off as soon as they exited those church doors? Church. Every Sunday morning. In many homes, there was never a doubt about the Sunday plans. In fact, Saturday nights were dedicated to preparing for Sunday: clothes laid out, the smell of burnt hair, and momma prepping Sunday dinner. A big deal. Sundays were indeed for church.

Starting the week in Sunday School was not taken lightly in most Christian homes. It was thoroughly enjoyable to learn about Jesus through catchy songs and Bible stories while coloring those erroneous animated depictions of Bible characters. Sunday School was the time for children to learn and participate. But oh, what a time and difference it was in morning worship.

Having a good seat for morning worship was essential. I did not want to be too close to the front because I couldn't really see what was happening behind me without being overly obvious and turning around to watch. I couldn't sit in the back row because Momma needed us up closer so we could "pay attention." So, settling for a middle row was the safest choice for showtime. As a child, sitting back and observing all this, what I then considered old people singing loudly, jumping up and down, and running around the church to some good ole' sounding music was nothing short of entertaining. Praising God in a radical way. The hand clapping. The feet stomping. The skilled tambourine players. The random screams and hollers of "Amen" and "Hallelujah" startled me half the time until I became very familiar with them. It was so familiar, in fact, that I knew when to expect it and exactly who to expect it from. It was all like clockwork to me. I learned it and could mimic it all. But what was it for, and what did it mean?

I couldn't begin to fathom the reason behind some women's screams or why they would weep profusely during prayer every Sunday. I often wondered why these women in church were so sad. I mean, why else would someone shed tears like this week after week if they were "happy"? My eight-year-old self had no clue. Praise break after praise break. Altar call after altar call. Service after service. Sunday after Sunday. Year after year. It became a routine. It was familiar. Church became tradition.

Everybody knows that Mother's Day and Easter Sunday are the most attended services of the year. Getting to church early on these Sundays is the smartest thing any regular attendee can do. People who don't go to church the whole year show up on Easter. They may have drifted from the church, but they haven't completely forgotten what Easter represents. Non-churchgoers come for this symbolic day. They arrive with the whole family and might even bring along some friends. Not only are they showing up, but they are also dressed to impress. New dresses and three-piece suits will fill the sanctuary. Record-breaking numbers of children are in the church. Most of the children wear bright colors and are extra chatty due to their excitement about the Easter poem they must read or the speeches they will recite. Some are even thrilled to have their parents in church to see their presentation that they worked hard to memorize. When you inhale, you catch a whiff of a distinct aroma filled with a blend of hairspray, numerous perfumes, and colognes flowing through the sanctuary, mixed with the scent of women who have been cooking a big dinner for their family to enjoy. We can't forget about the plastic candy-filled eggs hidden around the churchyard and those baskets full of goodies waiting for the children after the service. All of this is for what's supposed to be a day of remembering what Jesus did for us and our sins: the day God defeated death and rose from the dead. But it's what we were raised doing. Our parents did it, and their parents did it too. It was tradition.

All the grandmothers and mothers feel proud and honored to have their sons, daughters, and grandchildren sit with them on Mother's Day. All those tears and prayers she offered throughout the year for God to keep them safe—and for them to return to God—rang through her mind. On that one special Sunday, those prayers seemed close to being answered. Those mothers would give an extra praise and "Hallelujah" so that others, especially their family members, could notice how happy they were to have their children in the house of the Lord. All of this, just to not see them in church again until the next special holiday service. Every year, the pastor comes to the podium to deliver their best sermon on Mother's Day and Easter because, let's face it, they are trying to preach a word they hope will encourage non-churchgoers to reconsider and start returning. If they could reach just one.

Generation after generation, we place a lot of emphasis

on traditions, especially the tradition of ensuring we take our children to church. And of course, we should raise our kids to go to church because the Bible instructs us to train up a child, and when they are older, they won't depart. That scripture has been the reason and driving force behind why many families believe it is important to ensure their children attend church.

As I became an adult, life experiences began to show me more and more why I needed God. Situation after situation helped me start to understand how much God loves me. As I sought God more, I began to grasp those "old people's" worship, praises, prayers, and tears. Why didn't I know God this way as a child? As a child, I always had a love and reverence for God that I couldn't fully explain. However, I know that if I had personally known and comprehended who God was as a child, it would have saved me a lot of grief, heartache, and trouble. I would have enjoyed more years of truly experiencing what it means to have a real relationship with such a great God, rather than practicing a religion out of tradition. I know I am not alone. There are so many people who went to church faithfully as children. Week after week, multiple services every week. Sometimes, they complained to their parents that they didn't want to go. Many teenagers expressed their frustration, proclaiming that they couldn't wait to be grown so they wouldn't have to attend church if they didn't want to. But as long as we were in our parents' houses, we went to church on Sundays. Attending church throughout childhood without any real understanding of who God is or what all the "commotion" in church was about leaves room for much doubt, as there is no solid foundation.

When traditions are followed without question and without flexibility, it can make it hard for children to truly understand and appreciate their meaning. The severity of many traditions can be harmful when they prevent individuals from adapting to new circumstances. We witnessed this firsthand when the world shut down in March 2020. Many people lost their way because they could not attend church as they normally did. Similarly, many churches lost their influence because they couldn't adapt to the new norm of attending church non-traditionally online. Symbolically, I believe God shut down tradition for a bigger purpose.

If we are going to teach religious traditions to our children, especially this generation, we must be intentional in providing contexts and reasoning. We need to stop believing they are too young to understand. The world is teaching them things, and they understand fully. Some traditions should be preserved as they honor God. However, there are many traditions we uphold and pass down to our children that we don't even know why we do them or what they mean. We are merely following the "well, it's what my parents did" position. This mindset doesn't aid in developing our children's understanding and relationship with God.

Chapter Two
TRAINING "WILL"

*"Train up a child in the way he should go, and
when he is old, he will not depart from it."*

—PROVERBS 22:6, NKJV

L earning to ride a bike as a child is a significant achieve-
ment. One of my baby girl's goals for the year is to
learn how to ride a bike without training wheels. We asked
her how she could accomplish this, and she said Daddy
needed to help her practice every day. Profound. When we
train, it's something we will need to practice regularly.

The dictionary defines training as teaching a particular skill or behavior through practice and instruction over
time. When you are trained, you gain an understanding
of those practices and instructions. You recognize why
certain skills and behaviors are necessary. Training your

children in the Lord is much more than simply taking them to church; attending church alone is insufficient.

We know and believe that God's word cannot fail, and God does not lie. If His word states it, then it is true. Consider this: if attending church was the meaning of Proverbs 22:6, then children who regularly attended church would not stray from Christ. Attending church doesn't make a person a Christian. Raising a child in the church does not guarantee they will know God in a way that prevents them from departing.

Children who grow up and drift from the church ultimately don't fully understand who God is and how He is relevant to them. True training will keep them from departing from God. It will help them distinguish between God and the church. In fact, training will show children the importance of relationship over religion and tradition.

As parents, we should help our children understand who God is for them at any age. God is very relevant to our children throughout their lives. They need to realize that God is not just concerned about adults. In fact, I believe God cares deeply for our children since they are the next generation that will carry His word further. I am reminded of Mark's description of when Jesus was ministering and evangelizing; a multitude of children began to gather around Him. I can imagine that when the children arrived, they were extremely talkative and inquisitive, which is why the disciples felt overwhelmed and tried to send the children away. As a mother of two very curious children, I completely understand what the disciples were experiencing. However, Jesus became upset with the disciples because He wanted the children to come to Him. Jesus understood that children have the unique ability to teach adults much about the Kingdom of God and the truth of who God is. Jesus said in Matthew 18:3 that unless you change and become like little children, you will never enter the kingdom of heaven. There is something about the mindset, humility, and vulnerability that children possess, which allows them to see and obey God wholeheartedly. Therefore, nurturing that connection while they are children is vital.

Situations arise for everyone, regardless of age, and in all those instances, it is an opportunity to reveal how God and His word pertain to that very thing. We must never make our children feel like the things they face or deal with are meaningless or don't matter. No matter how small they may seem compared to adult issues, they matter to them. They concern them. So, if it concerns them, it surely concerns God, just as all your situations, no matter how big or small, concern God. When we take note of our children's concerns and help them bring it to Jesus, we have done them a great service. For one, we have shown them how to approach God in any situation that arises. We are showing them that God is, in fact, concerned about them. We are "showing" them that God is indeed the answer to their problem. We aren't just telling them; we are demonstrating how to get results from God.

Furthermore, when we teach our children to go directly to the Creator when issues arise in their lives, we equip them with a skill they will not forget. By allowing God to act on our children's behalf and involving them in the process, we provide them with personal experiences of who God is and what He can do. These experiences lead anyone to an understanding of God. The mistake many parents make is taking their children's issues to God themselves, thereby not allowing the child to engage in the process, which means the child isn't fully trained. You caught the fish for them, but didn't teach them how to fish for their future needs. Simply put, you prayed and got God to act for them, but didn't teach them to pray and seek God for themselves so they know how to when the next situation arises. You didn't train them; the opportunity for training was available but missed.

I remember one Thursday when my daughter, at the age of four, swallowed a nickel. After I attempted the Heimlich maneuver and saw her vomiting all over the place with no nickel in sight, we rushed to the emergency room. I was a wreck, mainly because I have a very weak stomach. The sight and smell of that vomit were overwhelming. But it was also the unknown that had my stomach in knots, literally worried sick. I didn't know what the outcome would be. I know children swallow things all the time, but not all these mishaps end the same way. Would surgery be required? Is her airway clear so she doesn't stop breathing? Will this nickel cause damage to my baby's insides? I was shaken. Fear of the unknown can cause so much unnecessary stress to you and those around you.

Putting my own thoughts and feelings aside, the fear in my daughter's eyes crushed me. She was terrified, and it showed. The healthcare personnel at the ER welcome desk checked us in, and my baby girl was still gagging and crying while we waited. While holding my daughter with a barf bag covering much of her face, I decided to pray. I had to settle these feelings and the fear that was not only overtaking me but was also rubbing off onto my children. More often than not, our emotions and struggles are unconsciously projected onto our children. Prayer was going to bring peace to both me and them and return us to the truth of what I believed and trusted God to do.

When I prayed, I didn't have to make a huge scene. Whenever I call on Jesus, whether loud or whispered, I am confident He hears my prayers. I had to pray because I knew at that moment, my children didn't need to see a frantic, fearful, faithless mother. They needed to see a mother who displayed the faith she told them they desperately needed in unknown times.

The nurse called my daughter's name so we could get an x-ray done. The x-ray technician, outside of his duties, made a crazy comment while viewing the monitor that invoked fear once again. Inside, my heart sank, but I kept a calm demeanor. I knew what I had just prayed, and I had to stand on that no matter what the unknown. So, the kids and I were sent back into the waiting area of the emergency room because there were still no available rooms. My daughter whispered to me, "Mommy, I'm scared." I began to assure her she didn't have to be afraid because God was with her. At that moment, my four-year-old child, sitting in a waiting room with countless strangers around, began to pray words of faith in her own words. She was bold and thanked God for making her better. That prayer was what she needed. She needed to seek God for herself, even though she heard me praying for her.

After she prayed, she smiled so brightly. She was lifted and comforted by God in her prayer. She told me immediately, "I'm going to be okay," and she began to sing and play as her normal self. She had noticeably stopped worrying and was no longer vomiting. She had wiped her tears, and fear was gone. Her faith in who God is to her was applied to her situation.

We waited a while longer for a room. Once we got into the room, another x-ray was done. At that point, we were told by the doctor, contrary to what the x-ray technician had said, that the nickel was in her stomach, and they advised us to give the coin time to potentially pass through her bowels on its own. The doctor instructed us to come back in three days if it hadn't passed. For three long days, every time she went to the bathroom, we prayed for it to pass. For three days, I, a very squeamish woman, searched the poop of my four-year-old looking and waiting for this nickel to show up. Each time I would say optimistically, "Nothing yet," and she would say, "It's going to come."

Take note of that word "yet." Our faith was aligned, and we agreed, so we believed that at some point, it was coming. My four-year-old and I were in full expectation of what we believed God for.

On Monday morning, we returned to the emergency room and had another x-ray done. While waiting, I honestly thought we had just missed it during one of our searches of the poop, and that the nickel was gone. However, that's not what we were told. The doctors explained that they needed to schedule surgery because the foreign object was still showing to be in the same place in the stomach. I couldn't understand this for the life of me because my daughter eats well and had been pooping frequently, so how could it be in the same place? Imagine the disappointment. I felt disappointed but still full of thankfulness and hope that my daughter would be just fine! The doctor provided me with the information I needed to schedule the surgery to have the nickel removed. I asked several questions. My questions were specifically meant for me to know what to discuss with God. I wanted to provide God with the details and specifics of what was going on. The doctor instructed me to try to get the surgery scheduled by the end of the week. When my daughter heard the word "surgery," she became sad. She said, "God is going to make it come out," and that she wouldn't need surgery. I assured her that even if she had to undergo surgery to remove the coin she swallowed, God would still be with her. However, that wasn't what her faith expressed. She was believing God for no surgery at all!

As a family, we decided to pray based on what my daughter was believing God for. Every night during our family dinner and prayer time, we said a special prayer just for our little Sunshine. On Thursday morning at 5:00 a.m., when I got up for my daily personal time with God, my daughter slid into my chair and sat with me. Normally, I would have walked her back to her room because this is my one-on-one time with God. However, on this particular day, I decided just to let her stay, as I figured she would fall asleep anyway. I continued to pray and meditate as she sat quietly. At 6:30 a.m., the children's "wake-up" alarm went off so they could get up for school. As I went to my son's room to wake him, my daughter disappeared into the bathroom. I went on with our morning routine of getting dressed, fixing lunches and breakfast, and getting the kids' things together.

In the same way she had been doing since day one of our search for the coin, my daughter yelled, "Mom, I pooped!" so I could check it for the nickel. One squeeze and CLACK—the sound of metal hit the bottom of the toilet. "Hallelujah!" I screamed. Immediately, my son started walking through the house, thanking God for answering his earnest prayers for his sister. My daughter laughed and jumped up and down, saying, "God did it." We FaceTimed my husband, and my children excitedly told their dad the amazing news. For ten minutes, my children and I praised and worshipped God together for answering our prayers. We ended up being late for school and work, but it didn't matter. I was able to allow my children to experience God and see Him work for them in their own situations. They were able to praise and worship God in their own way outside of the church. My children were able to understand that God is relevant to them. I know that is one situation my daughter will never forget. This situation gave her personal knowledge of what prayer, faith, and God can do for her. It is the personal experience and knowledge of God that makes us want Him more. Church alone could never have given her this experience and knowledge. The training in this situation gave her a better understanding of God.

When we fully understand the love and power of God, we wouldn't ever want to leave Him. That's why truly training a child in the way of God is important; they will not depart from Him. They won't leave God because they will not want to leave. That personal experience is something the church can't teach. Simply going to church doesn't help a person, especially a child, fully experience the love of God, the power of God, or learn to love and obey God. Going to church is where we have the opportunity to express our love, honor, and thankfulness for God collectively with others who believe in Him as we do. It allows us to hear the word of God so that we can apply it to our lives when we are away from the church.

Chapter Three
HIDE & SEEK

"How can young people keep their lives pure? By obeying your word. I have tried hard to find you — don't let me wander from your commands. I have hidden your word in my heart, that I might not sin against you."

—PSALM 119:9-11, NLT

One of my favorite things to do is sit back and watch my children play hide and seek. Hide and seek is a household favorite in our home. Everyone hides while one person is the seeker. The seeker counts to 10, 20, or whatever number they decide at that moment, while everyone tries to find the best hiding spot. It's always so funny how my little four-year-old will go to the most obvious spots and giggle the entire time until she is found. It didn't take my kids long to learn how to play this game. They started playing around two years old and picked up the concept quickly.

Children have a significant advantage. They possess a remarkable ability to adopt new habits and learn quickly due to several factors. Children's brains are like sponges. Their brains are highly plastic, which means they have a greater capacity for forming and reorganizing neural connections. This facilitates the acquisition of new skills and knowledge. Their brain structures are still developing, and their neural pathways are more malleable, allowing for rapid learning. There is nothing they hear that they cannot repeat. And even if they do not repeat it, they definitely remember it and think about it. How often have you heard your toddler use a big word and wonder where they learned it? It's simple. They heard it on a television show, or they heard you say it a few weeks ago, and waited for the perfect moment to use the word they added to their vocabulary. If children see something done enough times, they will unconsciously reenact it. I think about the smallest hand gestures I make or the facial expressions I show in certain situations and find my children doing the exact same thing in sync with me. Clearly, they mimic because they believe this is the appropriate way to respond to this specific situation. Children learn and adopt behaviors effortlessly and swiftly. It does not take them long at all. For this reason, we must be very careful about what we say and do around them. Not just careful, but intentional.

I believe one of the top responsibilities of a parent is to prepare our children for their future and to help them handle life as well-rounded, independent adults. In raising children who truly understand who God is, we must assist them in learning scriptures that they can hide in their hearts. There are many Christians serving God who lack a true understanding of who He really is. They don't know His characteristics, nor what His word says about their situations. They have no real sense of the love He genuinely has for them. Christians settle in their lives because they don't understand how the word of God can be applied to their lives, offering them more than they could imagine.

As parents, most of us desire to give our children what we didn't have. We want to help them avoid the mistakes we made. Parents typically want to teach their children the lessons learned through tough life experiences. If I could teach my children all the lessons I learned from my heartbreaks, disappointments, and failures, I would, just to help them avoid what I dealt with. Now I know they will have to face their own trials, but I don't think they have to repeat mine. So, if I can help them understand some of the many things I have found God to be personally over the years, I want to do that. I long for my children to develop their own personal relationship with God and set aside the entire thought of religion. My parents talked about God, but they never made it personal or relevant to me in my younger days. My dad's favorite thing to say was, "You need God." But I didn't fully understand that until I became an adult.

Many people are stuck in teaching religion instead of teaching relationship. I believe this is mainly because it's hard to explain something to someone when you don't fully understand it yourself. As a child, my parents were religious. We did many things out of tradition. I know my parents loved God, but many of their beliefs were based on what the church was teaching or its doctrine and weren't necessarily biblical. Of course, experience, studying, and building that relationship played a huge role in them learning more about God, allowing them to correct some wrongs and start encouraging us to "just get close to Jesus."

My father loved God deeply. I mean, he spoke about God and his amazement at Him all the time. My dad never got tired of sharing his thoughts and feelings about who God was to him. After my mom divorced my dad when I was about 12, we developed a really close relationship. During that low and dark time in his life, my dad experienced God on a different level. Before the divorce, he was stern and strict about what he believed was the right way. There was little room for grace in many areas. It wasn't until after this difficult period that my dad began explaining in great detail who he understood God to be, sharing specific details of his personal experiences that showed how only God brought him out of those situations. My dad's compassion and open heart emerged after he truly got to know God for himself. When you truly know Jesus, there's no way you can remain unchanged. You cannot follow religion when you come to the knowledge of God. Throughout my teenage years into adulthood, my dad taught me so much about who God is. I grew not just to love God, but I desired to know Him personally like my dad did. When someone you love, admire, and trust—a parent—is bragging about this undeniable love and closeness they have with God, it makes you want to pursue that as well.

Children trust their parents. The younger they are, the more they trust the opinions and thoughts of their parents. Teenagers tend to lean towards the "parents don't know anything" stage, but believe me when I say they are still listening, watching, and considering your perspective. While you have your child's attention and influence over their beliefs, why not pour as much as you can into them? Teach them how to hide the word of God in their hearts and seek God and His ways for themselves.

Many parents cover their children in prayer and speak the scriptures to and over them. I simply believe that we also must help them learn to do this for themselves. I enjoy directing my children to scriptures that will help them in the everyday situations they face at their age. When your children get sick, direct them to THE HEALER. Get the Bible or open your Bible app on your phone and search God's word for scriptures about healing. Children who are smart enough to ask Siri questions can most definitely ask her, "What does the Bible say about healing?" Google is an amazing search engine that can be used if you do not know exactly which scriptures apply to what they are facing at that moment. There is also a search tool in a Bible app that can help guide you or your child. The point is to teach them how to search, so when they find themselves in tough situations without you, they can go straight to the source, the Word of God.

Recite applicable scriptures with your child. Ask them which of the scriptures you just read they liked the best. This allows them to grasp it, keep it in their heart and mind, and understand how it applies to their own life. You can also choose one of the scriptures that is written simply and help them learn that scripture by heart. This practice helps them when they face a similar situation; they will automatically think of the scripture they memorized and understood. Trust me, they will remember it! Kids learn these catchy songs with one listen; they can memorize a scripture, too. If you have them repeat it more than three times, that scripture will enter their minds and hearts. After they memorize a scripture, I like to ask them for their thoughts. I will ask them to share what they think that scripture means, and I will go even further by asking if they believe it. This practice allows them to go beyond just hearing Bible stories. It gives them the ability to think about and analyze what they've read. When they have the word hidden in their hearts, it makes it harder to walk away from God. When they have the word in their hearts, they will know the scripture that provides clear direction when making decisions, helping them because they will understand and obey God's word. It's hard to obey something you do not know. With the word in their hearts, they can remind themselves of what God says as situations arise.

I love what the word explains in Psalm 119. Verse nine

poses a question, asking how a young person can keep his life clean or pure. Instructions follow the question: 1) take heed to God's word, 2) seek after God so you don't drift away from His commandments, 3) hide God's word in your heart to keep yourself from sinning against God. Learning, comprehending, and believing scriptures early in life helps to keep children from traveling down sinful and dark roads as they grow older. When we don't have the word already in our hearts, we face and deal with things that could have been avoided. We go down a road of destruction due to ignorance. Don't allow your children to be unaware of the ways the enemy can lead them off track and down a path that God never intended for them.

As a child, my favorite scripture was Ephesians 6:1-4. I knew that scripture by heart at a very early age and would recite it often. If it were Youth Sunday at church and I had been assigned to read the scripture for the service, I would always read Ephesians 6:1-4. I could flip right to it in any Bible. Even better, I could stand up there without a Bible and recite it word for word as if I were reading directly from it. As a child, I felt this scripture was relevant to me. I felt it in my bones when I read it. I remember the fear of upsetting God by not obeying my parents. Every single time I read or heard that scripture, I applied it to little ol' me! That scripture made me want to honor and obey my parents. I had dissected it and truly hid it in my heart. Having that scripture hidden in my heart prevented me from rebelling against or disrespecting my parents because I knew the promise of God attached to it. As I got older and became a teen, I had no desire to go against my parents. Not because I was afraid of them or couldn't, but simply because the words of Ephesians 6 rang so loudly in my head; if I didn't honor and obey them, my days would be shortened, and my life would be cut short. I had dreams and goals. I didn't want my life cut short. I didn't want to die because I didn't honor or obey my mom and dad. I was not that girl. I wanted to live my whole life completely.

As I got older, I started to realize that the "days shortened, or life cut short" didn't always necessarily mean death. It also meant that while living, your days of freedom may be cut short (incarceration) or, even if you weren't incarcerated, you won't have peace in your life; you will be existing and not living. I found that this also dealt with the quality of life you would have if you didn't honor your mother and father.

Chapter Four
LET THAT DIGEST

"And He said to me, 'Son of man, feed your belly, and fill your stomach with this scroll that I give you.' So, I ate, and it was in my mouth like honey in sweetness."

—EZEKIEL 3:3, ESV

I remember when I was a child, so many kids would be dropped off at the church for midweek service and Sunday morning worship, week after week, and I had no idea who their parents were. Growing up in what I thought was a strict home environment, I found it pretty cool that they were trusted to go anywhere without their parents. As I got older and assumed a more responsible role as a youth leader, I recalled all the children who would catch the church bus to come to church without their parents. At that time, I learned many of these kids genuinely enjoyed attending service and weren't necessarily being "forced"; it was often an escape for them. One thing that remained the same in both time periods was that many of the parents sending their children to church had actually been raised to go to church themselves; they just didn't attend anymore.

Many of the services held at my home church while I was growing up always involved food. For Sunday School, they often served breakfast. Snacks and drinks were either provided after the service or sold for fundraising. Many Black churches' main fundraisers were dinner sales: Fried Chicken Sale, BBQ Chicken and Ribs Sale, and let's not forget the Bake Sale. The major events, such as Family and Friends Day, Pastor's Anniversary, or Pack-a-Pew, all featured a full dinner menu. You know the good ole' fried chicken, green beans, rice, rolls, soda, and a slice of pound cake dinner. Having something to fill the bellies of the attendees seemed ideal after or before they receive their "spiritual food" from the service.

And think, even if the church wasn't serving food after service, Sunday dinner was most definitely waiting on the stove for many, and local buffet restaurants were packed with saints just coming from church. I know most, while sitting in church with the preacher on his third closing, were really thinking about the dinner they were about to eat. Bellies were rumbling. The food was calling. I'm talking about a good homecooked Sunday dinner that included mac-n-cheese, cabbage, rice, candied yams, roast beef, fried chicken, cornbread, and some lemon-flavored sweet tea. And before that food can even digest, you fall into the gracious Sunday afternoon nap. But what about the word of God we received? Did we consume that properly to even have it digest?

Digestion is vital to the human body. To digest something means to break it down into substances that can be absorbed and used by the body. As it relates to understanding, it means to read or hear new information and take the necessary time to comprehend it. Digestion is important to our physical bodies because it breaks food down into nutrients, which the body uses for energy, growth, and cell repair. A baby wouldn't be able to eat a piece of steak and digest it properly. That meat would have to be ground and processed into a puree that would allow the baby to consume it.

This is the same in the spiritual realm; we must all digest the word. Our children's minds, souls, and bodies are not fully developed. They often don't understand the things of God, or the messages preached or taught. Many can't even explain why they go to church or what is happening during the service. If we are being completely honest, many adults are sitting in church today without a clue as to what is really going on. They just know it is a good service. This is simply due to no one taking the time to break it down for them so they could fully understand it for themselves.

Digestion for children is especially important. Children have limited cognitive abilities and may struggle to grasp complex ideas as they are presented by a preacher who doesn't have the gift of "teaching." By breaking down spiritual concepts into simpler, age-appropriate terms, children can better understand and connect with the ideas being presented. This helps bridge the gap between their developmental level and the depth of spiritual concepts. If you think about the Biblical stories you learned as a child and revisit them as an adult, the concepts and spiritual meaning mean more now. You understand them differently as an adult than you did as a child. Life experiences, development, and spiritual maturity allow one to gain more from spiritual ideas and concepts than what we could understand as children.

That's why I believe Children's Church is important. In the main service, the word is delivered by preachers and pastors who often engage in more hard breathing and hollering than taking the time to make spiritual concepts simplistic and straightforward. Less than half of the adults in the congregation can fully follow and understand the message, so children most definitely aren't receiving the word of God explained at their level of understanding. Lives aren't transformed when a person can't grasp the word in a way that allows them to apply it to their own lives. For your child to digest the word of God and all that it is meant to do in their lives, it must not be complex and should be simplified for them.

There are countless things, truly everything, that children need parents to break down into ways they can comprehend. Understanding enables them to grow spiritually, gaining deeper insight into who God is. When they grasp it, they too can apply that knowledge in their lives when needed. What we help them digest becomes part of their essence, their being, and their soul.

As I stated in the chapter entitled "Traditions," children are observing, watching, and listening to many things while attending church services. I believe it is crucial for parents and guardians to attend services with their children. By being there with your children, you have the chance to explain further and help them relate to what is taught and demonstrated during services. Children should understand why communion is taken and its significance. Even if you don't know the specifics, when the sacrament of reconciliation is performed and scriptures are read, you gain some understanding and can explain it to your children. This understanding enables them to partake in communion not just out of tradition or ritual, but with a heart that remembers exactly what Jesus Christ did for them [us all] when He died for our sins, helping them recognize why this is indeed very important as Christians.

It is the same for baptism. Your children should understand why people are baptized and what it means to be baptized. When my son asked to be baptized, I wouldn't agree until he could explain why he wanted to be baptized and what it meant to him. I wanted him to grasp the seriousness of being baptized and not just do it because he thought it was cool to get in the church's pool. By the time the day came for his baptism, he was so emotional and thankful for the opportunity because he understood what baptism meant for him and to him.

So often, we take things lightly and make them trivial, which fosters an attitude in our children about those very things. These children grow into adults who share the same perspective. Now, we face another generation that is religious but lacks real substance, understanding, and, most importantly, a relationship with Christ. Consider something your parents didn't view as a big deal when you were young, and now you hold those same views.

Breaking down what happens in church is fundamental for the growth and understanding of children (or anyone, for that matter) who desire a true relationship with Christ and plan to stay connected to their faith. It is this breakdown of concepts and ideas that allows the substance to be absorbed and appreciated. Many don't believe in separating children during service, but we are blessed to attend a church that has a children's church. They are taught at their age and maturity level. One of the first things we do upon leaving church service is ask each of our children what they learned in their youth class during Children's Church. Each child gets a chance to teach the family from their own perspective about what they learned. If they are slightly off, we always redirect them and explain further without taking away from what they were taught in the class. We love this time because it opens their minds and prevents them from leaving church thinking it was just something to do, or that it wasn't for them. The main question I am sure to ask is,

"How can you apply this to your life?" If they can apply it, they have digested it. We further engage by letting them ask questions about things they didn't understand. It is a chance for us to explain the word in a way that helps them better understand, giving them that one-on-one lesson of breaking down what they had just received at church. If your church has a children's church, allow your children to attend. For pastors reading this, I challenge you to start a children's church ministry so that these children aren't leaving service week in and week out without receiving a message they understand.

When the kids are in the main service listening to the pastor teach or preach, they don't always fully understand what he is saying. My husband and I like to break it down for our little ones so they can grasp the message. I've found that doing this right after service, during those drives home, is best because the message and spiritual concepts are fresh in our minds. It's hard to remember the context of something days later without rewatching it if it happens to be recorded. This is one of my favorite activities with my children. The best part of these recaps with them is when I later hear them discussing things we've talked about regarding the word or praying about things they heard at church days or weeks later. This lets me know they aren't just going to church to watch; they are learning and digesting what is being taught about God and their faith.

Referencing past messages when things arise with one of the kids during the week is another practice we maintain. When you can refer back to what was taught and help the child apply the sermon to their specific situation as it occurs, it enhances their understanding of that message even more. This practice of helping your children process what happens in church and the messages preached will be something they thank you for in the future. Take the time to help your children truly digest what they take from the service. No concept is too small. Ask them open-ended questions about the service. Listen carefully to understand what they are saying so you can respond. It is crucial to acknowledge the parts they do understand. When the child seems to grasp the concept, extend the discussion by asking how it can be applied to their own life or why the concept is important. Don't overwhelm them and avoid making it too complex. Just as putting too much food in your mouth at once makes it harder to chew and swallow, the same principle applies to someone trying to read, understand, and discuss too much information at once. It will be too challenging to comprehend and process fully. So, discuss it just enough for them to have thoughts to ponder and gain a full understanding. Make this enriching time exciting for them, like a momma doing the airplane to get her baby to open his mouth for baby food. Be sure to revisit the discussion a few days later. Whatever you do, don't leave your child to choke on the word and try to figure it out for themselves. Find a way to puree, grind, and help them process the things of God.

Chapter Five
A NEGLECTED CHILD

"But those who won't care for their relatives, especially those in their own household, have denied the true faith. Such people are worse than unbelievers."

—1 TIMOTHY 5:8, NLT

When people think of the word neglect, they automatically assume it refers to a parent's failure to provide sufficient supervision or basic needs, such as food and shelter, for a child. However, neglect is more than that. In this chapter, I will break down the forms of neglect as they relate to spirituality. This is my attempt to help parents understand how a child or teenager can experience spiritual neglect from a parent, which can lead to them departing from God. This discussion strictly concerns spiritual neglect. In most cases, spiritual neglect is not intentional or even recognizable. Most parents are simply doing what they were taught, attempting to do their best with what they have. Yet, people perish (die) from lack of knowledge. When revelation comes, we must do better and change our approach. God gave me this revelation as a new mom, and He has now released me to share it with the world. It is time for us to move beyond what was passed down to us and embrace what God needs for this generation of parents. The upcoming generation cannot afford to experience the unintentional spiritual neglect that many have suffered through.

Many adults are victims of spiritual neglect and don't even realize it or understand what it truly entails. Spiritual neglect is the failure to properly nurture an individual's spirituality or soul, leaving the soul neglected. It specifically refers to a lack of attention, care, or support provided to one's spiritual well-being or religious beliefs. This neglect occurs when a person's spiritual needs, practices, or beliefs are overlooked, leading to feelings of emptiness, disconnection, or a sense of spiritual unfulfillment.

First, let's address a word that I believe is key here: the word "properly." I will reiterate that many parents are doing the best they can with what they have, what they know, and what they have been taught. Not everything they have learned is the best or proper, but that is what they can provide.

Admittedly, I am a bit of a perfectionist. I live by doing everything "as unto the Lord." I just refuse to give God any ole' thing. So, in everything, I try to operate in excellence.

When I became a mother, I wanted to not just settle for what I was taught or already knew from others. I started seeking God and praying about being a great mother to the blessing that God sent me. I began reading more books about parenting and studying the word to help me understand this important role as a mother. Raising children is no easy task, but I wanted to do it with excellence. God started giving me more and more wisdom about children and raising them. Before I even had children, I would share my thoughts and advise my sisters and friends when they encountered different situations with their children. Even at this early stage of life, when giving parenting advice, I would always try to downplay my comments because I wasn't even a mom, so how could I know? Then I started to believe that God was revealing things to me in preparation for my role in my future children's lives, so that I could raise them as unto the Lord. Now I understand the bigger assignment was in preparation for Him releasing this revolutionary book for this generation of parents of the next generation.

Proper care refers to appropriate and effective support, attention, and treatment. Every child is different. What is appropriate and effective for one child is not necessarily the same for another. In understanding this, you should know that as generations change, children change. They are wiser, and laws and societal views have changed. What worked in the 60s doesn't necessarily work for these new age children. Many children are suffering from spiritual neglect because parents are failing to care for their child's spirituality properly, attempting to use the methods of care that their parents and grandparents used in their time. To care for the spirituality of the child properly, you must be keen on what they are lacking and what type of attention and support is needed. This is not the time to allow pride to create an "I know what my kids need" attitude. Often, we don't know how our children feel because we don't give them a voice or space to share with us what is going on with them. My first course of action is always to go to the Creator. He created them, so He knows all about them. Allow God to give you wisdom on discovering what is lacking in your child's spiritual life. What will play the biggest part in being able to do this is where we, as parents, are spiritually. Some may not have a strong spiritual foundation of their own, while others are so wrapped up in church and serving that they fail to spiritually nurture their own children.

On one side of spiritual neglect, there are children or teens who are spiritually neglected simply by being left to figure God out for themselves. I've heard people say, "You just have to learn who God is and decide what you will believe for yourself." These children have little to no guidance and are forced to piece together a concept of who God is, what they can fully comprehend enough to believe, and have no one to go to for in-depth explanations or to ask questions. These are often the kids who are dropped off at church by parents who were once compelled to attend church as children themselves. These parents fail to understand the significance of showing their child just how important it is to follow God.

Although it is a great starting place for ensuring your children are raised in the church, when your child knows you once regularly attended church as a minor and then decided at some point along the way to stop going, for whatever reason, it unintentionally sends the message that "church is for kids and real old people." As a child, why would anyone want to follow and believe in Jesus if they don't see their own parents doing so? Neglecting their spirituality by sending them to church while not displaying the same need suggests that you want them to attend church just to figure out that they don't need God. That is one of the worst messages to send to a developing individual.

We must practice what we teach. If we send our children to church and expect them to understand that God is important and that they need Him, they must also see us, as parents and adults, needing God and recognizing His importance in our lives. If God deserves your children's time, He should also deserve your time as a parent. Simply sending your kids to church while you do not attend with them is not enough. This generation is not accepting that nor are they passively agreeing with, "that is just how it is." This practice or method of making children believe they need God as youth but not as adults has created generations of people who know of God but do not have a lasting relationship with Him. Parents have imparted harmful messages that have resulted in cycles of children growing into adults with the same mindset. Some of these unintentional messages that have cultivated dangerous spiritual mindsets are: "Church is for kids and real old people," "Go to church as a child because your parent says so, but when you are grown, you don't have to," and "You need church, but I don't." We all need God. Our children need to see us want and need God just as much as we want them to. Don't send these messages through your actions by not attending church with your children. Build your relationship with Christ as an adult while your children watch. Park your car and walk into the sanctuary with your child rather than just dropping them off. There is nothing so bad that you have done that can keep you away from the love of God. If this is you, take the step and get back to church, not because you must go or are being forced by your parents, but because you desire to go and realize that you need God.

On another side of spiritual neglect is a group of church and ministry leaders' children. No one knows how often the children of pastors and leaders are unintentionally neglected. Leaders often overlook their own children because they fail to recognize that there could be a lack in their own families. Many believe their children are better off compared to those being dropped off at church or those dealing with serious family issues, who, as church leaders, they tend to spend most of their time counseling and evangelizing. Leaders mistakenly think their children don't need them as much or in the same ways as their flock or those they are serving in the ministry.

Studies suggest that a significant portion of pastors' kids, around 33%, are no longer actively attending church, and 7% no longer consider themselves Christian. Many preachers' kids have dealt with feelings of being unheard and unseen, and that their parents are needed by others more than they have time to give to them as children. Not to mention, learning about and experiencing how church folks behave, along with watching how it affects their parents, causes resentment towards the church, and ultimately, the church becomes equated with God. While nurturing the children in the church you lead as a pastor or vital ministry leader, you must actively include your own children. Don't assume that just because they are yours, they have no issues and are getting everything they need. The truth is that the enemy is attacking them twice as much because they are connected to you.

Many church leaders make their kids miss out on being children (enjoying sports and extracurricular activities) so that they have the time to be at the "church" as much as possible to serve. My husband and I are both PKs (Preacher's Kids). He frequently mentions how he missed out on a lot as a child due to his dad's belief that "church" was more important. He recalls the basketball games he missed because his dad didn't want him to miss church on weekdays. My husband relives the regret of not being involved in school sports because of his father's and ultimately his own responsibility to the church. This has bothered him for years and caused some resentment towards "church responsibility and leadership roles." I mean, he legitimately shies away from having any title or role because he believes it will take away from his family. Scarred, but we are still praying! Very early in our relationship, I was clear that church could and would never come before our marriage or our children, and that we would take God with us everywhere. In the beginning, I can say this was a little hard for him to grasp fully. In his mind, church and God were one and the same. Missing a church service for a vacation with his new wife was tough and often out of the question. It was once we started having children that I believe he began to understand my stance. My husband's motto and what he lives by is "God, wife, kids, and everything/everybody else." We had a mutual agreement that we wouldn't limit our children's lives and their childhood just to keep up with what the church had going on. The truth was that the church always had something going on. Now, with two children, we've managed to have them heavily involved in sports and activities while remaining very active in church ministry. If there is ever a conflict in schedule, we involve them in deciding whether we will skip a game for service or if we will catch the next service so they can attend their game.

Oftentimes, the children of pastors and church leaders serve the church, shouldering heavy responsibilities at a young age. My husband, as the pastor's son, was the keyboard player for the church from the age of 10 and later became the minister of music. He felt he couldn't miss a service; if he weren't there, there would be no music. Simultaneously, he believed there was no other purpose for his church attendance other than to provide the best music possible. Thus, he felt an overwhelming responsibility to the ministry, but he also wasn't receiving the spiritual nourishment he needed because he was constantly in the service zone. Early on, he learned that serving the ministry often meant sacrificing his own needs, leading to a form of spiritual starvation. This heavy realization became ingrained in him, making it difficult to release that mindset. Once he freed himself from it, he fell in love with discovering God for himself. I'm not a doctor, but I suspect some resentment lingered as well. Missing out on many things he wished to do in his youth likely contributes to his hesitance to serve in ministry since leaving his parents' church. There is trauma rooted in the sacrifices made in being a leader.

On the other hand, I was raised in a household where we were encouraged to be kids, as my parents wanted to ensure we had that experience. Don't get me wrong; we were in church all the time, attending multiple services a week. However, I never missed softball games, cheer events, or school activities. When I became a parent, my dad noticed the many roles I was taking on in the church and often reminded me to ensure our kids could participate in the activities they wanted and to invest in our children. One day, when I mentioned my son was going to miss a practice due to a church engagement, my dad, the pastor, told me, "There are people at the football field who need to know God and see God in you." He added, "Don't confine your calling to the four walls of the church. Let God use you in other arenas. Why limit your ministry to just the 'church'?" He reminded me that once childhood opportunities are missed, they won't come back.

If you have children who want to play community sports or engage in non-church activities, use opportunities in the community, arenas, and audiences to show or share Christ with others. Let your children see you take God into any environment and demonstrate how they can love God while pursuing their dreams, even if it means missing a church meeting. Teach them that Christians may not always surround them, but they can still be a light in those settings. I love wearing Christian shirts or hats to my children's sporting events because they often spark conversations with complete strangers. Allowing your children to enjoy their youth while discovering their God-given abilities and talents teaches them how to live a balanced life. I know many PKs (pastor's kids) who left the church because they didn't understand or appreciate how the church could consume all their time, leaving no room for anything else. They watched their parents devote themselves to the ministry, never taking a vacation or missing gatherings or fun activities. But that isn't the will of God. God desires for His people to have life and to have it more abundantly. An abundant life includes time for resets, enjoying family away from church, and participating in activities that bring joy. Allowing children to grow resentful of the church because you failed to notice they needed to learn how to balance serving and personal time is truly a disservice.

The scripture says we fail in faith if we do not care for and provide for our own families, especially those within our homes. The Bible states that these are the worst kinds of people. I would assert that these are the worst kinds of Christians. Don't neglect your children's needs; they can't always articulate what they require. As believers and parents, we must seek God concerning our children. I'm constantly asking God how to parent or address situations with my kids. My two children live in the same home and have the same parents. They were raised with the same morals and beliefs, yet they have different needs. So, we respond to each of them differently while ensuring their needs are met. Part of providing for their needs includes understanding when they may desire to participate in sports because it could be a dream or talent God has given them, and they need to develop those skills. It might also involve the need to be heard, understood, and seen, as well as to have your undivided attention outside of your role as pastor, youth leader, minister, or whatever. They simply need mom and dad. Learn to separate your role as a parent from your role at the church. I can't tell you how many teens and young adults experience the heartbreaking moment when their parents approach a situation in their lives as a pastor or church leader, rather than as a loving mom or dad.

Chapter Six
WHAT CHRIST-LIKE LOOKS LIKE

"Imitate me, just as I imitate Christ."
—1 CORINTHIANS 11:1, NKJV

B eing "Christlike" refers to qualities, characteristics, and behaviors like those of Christ. These attributes are supposed to define Christianity. Our everyday lives, how we behave, react, and live day to day, should be a direct reflection of Christ. Being a Christian means not only believing in Jesus Christ but also living as Christ did. What happens outside those church walls truly shows the world, and your children, who Christ is in your life. Are you real or fake? It's a hard reality. We are setting an example, and they are mentally storing images of how to act in different situations or how they should carry themselves. Most people who stray from the church often believe that churchgoers are hypocrites or fake. Those who remain with God often have strong examples of Christianity. If we live a life outside the church that pleases Christ, our children will naturally see the love we have for Him and will be more inclined to nurture that love for Him themselves.

We have all heard people say that Christians are some of the most hypocritical individuals. Don't contribute to that generalization. Make it your heart's desire to be a living example and truly live out this Christ-like life. The fact is that our children are watching us more than we realize. As parents, we set the tone in our homes. When situations arise, notice how our children wait to see how we respond. We've discussed that children mimic their parents. If you want to know how others view you, observe your children, because most of the time, they act and respond very similarly to you. This is yet another hard truth.

I think about how my kids, especially my 10-year-old son, somehow have road rage, even though they don't drive. I remember a car pulling out in front of me, and they both were in complete uproar. They were yelling and throwing their hands in the air. My daughter was saying, "Go faster, mommy; catch up." After I dropped them off at school, I reflected on this and could only think about all the times I have grunted and screamed, "Get out of the way," "What are you doing," or "What in the world," as drivers failed to follow the rules of the road. So, it was clear why they respond this way when they see drivers and cars doing things I have reacted to in similar situations. It's amusing that they know exactly when and how to react, even though they have never driven a car or even been behind the wheel to experience the frustration from bad drivers; yet, they react as if they understand what it feels like to be impacted and annoyed by these inconsiderate drivers. This is a clear example of children observing their parents over the years and then acting and responding in the same way they've witnessed.

Now think about the worst behavior or reaction you have displayed over time that you wouldn't want to see your own child doing. *Wheeeew.* This is why we must watch how we behave when we are teaching our children to live a righteous life. We don't want them to pick up behaviors and habits from us as parents that contradict the Christian life we portray at church. Our children follow our example, so we should be sure to follow Christ's example.

This is not to say that we won't make mistakes. Our children should see us make mistakes. They should also witness us correcting those mistakes and openly repenting when we mess up so that they understand the normality of Christians needing God's grace and mercy and possessing a heart of repentance. This will help them in their own lives. God absolutely expects us to follow His ways, but He also knows we are not perfect, fall short, and need His grace. What is important in demonstrating to our children what "Christ-like" looks like is living out the principles and concepts we are teaching them, so they don't hear us saying one thing while living something different. Show them what it means to be a Christian. If you are teaching your children always to trust God, you must illustrate that in your own life. When the toughest situations arise, show them how you aren't moved and how you stand on the promises of God. Let them see and hear you praying, reminding God of His word pertaining to that situation. It's okay to show your kids that you grow weary, but also how you always turn back to God. They need to observe what this looks like so that they can mimic it in their own lives when challenges arise. As they get older, the situations will become more serious and harder, but they will have a strong foundation and understanding of what it means to trust God. Don't let your children hear you proclaiming your trust in God while engaging in actions that contradict that trust and digging yourself into a deeper hole, making the situation worse.

Teaching your kids to treat people in the way Christ instructs us—to love and respect everyone, regardless of their background or differences—is so important. God's greatest commandment is to LOVE. If we are going to show anyone what it means to be Christ-like, we must start with love. Jesus loved this world so much that He laid down His life for the sins of everyone. We can't teach or show who or what Jesus Christ is if we don't know how to love others, no matter what. Even when people aren't very lovable, we can still love them. They should understand that you can love a person deeply while not agreeing with or supporting their wrong actions.

When my son was nine years old, we took him out for baseball assessments on a nice, cool evening in the small city of DeLand. He was so excited and ready to be back on the diamond field. All the kids were out on the field in a straight line, waiting for their turn to show the coaches what they could do in hopes of being recruited. My husband and I watched from the open fence. Something in me didn't feel right, so I didn't sit down, but I tried to blame it on nerves for my child. I saw the boys on the field talking and laughing. My attention was locked in on the field. I noticed my son and this little boy talking, and then my son moved closer. Before I knew it, I saw the kid swing at my son and miss, and then my son slammed him. I screamed my son's name and started running onto the field, but before I knew it, he had punched the kid in the face. I was so hurt and confused because this was just so out of character for him. Once I made it to the boys, I hysterically asked my son, "Why did you do that?" Standing there with my arms open waiting for some type of explanation as soon as he opened his mouth to say, "He called me a nigger. I told him to stop. I told him the word was offensive and disrespectful, but he said it again," I could hear the hurt in my baby boy's nine-year-old voice. I turned to the little boy and asked him why he would call him that. Before the little boy could respond, my son and I were surrounded by a bunch of white men screaming that he was kicked out and we needed to leave. My son kept trying to explain to them what happened, but they wouldn't listen to him. I decided

I couldn't allow my boiling flesh to make me act crazy in front of my son because he was visibly angry. I honestly was very proud of myself and the growth because the old me would have set it off on the field. But I chose to "let God" and we turned in my son's number and left, even though the other kid wasn't ridiculed or kicked out for using racial slurs. Now, granted, we did have a conversation with my son about controlling his anger and not turning to violence. But as a black man and woman, his dad and I fully understood what he felt inside. As a family, we discussed the situation. We explained to our son that we understood his anger and reaction, but this was a time for us as a family to forgive and show love to these people who may not have experienced or seen love from a different race. We let him hear our disapproval of what happened to him, validated him, and let him see us go into action on his behalf in a Godly way, which was led in a way of love and correction, not hate and retaliation.

The next morning, I allowed my son to post about this experience on social media. He went viral by noon. Then the president of the Little League organization reached out. With much love, I was able to voice my dismay. I openly expressed and explained how their handling of the situation was unacceptable and didn't convey a message of racial intolerance. A few days later, my family and I were asked to sit at a table with the board and the family of the other child. At this table, we educated and spoke directly and openly to a group of white individuals. There was no yelling, name-calling, or belittling. If there was any pre-conceived notion of what "our kind" was like, we had the opportunity to change that. The league ultimately decided not to punish my son and allowed him to remain in the league. We had the chance to discuss with our son how, in a world full of hate, we still have the choice to love as Christ instructs us. There is so much more to this story, but I left out many details and summarized things for the sake of time. The entire incident and its surrounding circumstances could really be a book in and of itself. But what I love most about it is how it went viral. The majority of the comments were about how well we handled the situation and how well-spoken my son was for his age. Many commented on how evident it is that we are raising our son well and that he managed the racial situation better than most adults. So not only did my son and the city witness us display Christ and respond with the intention of giving God the glory, but the world also got to see it.

So many times, we've talked to our son about handling situations with grace, love, and patience. It was in this tough incident that he saw it with his eyes wide open because it involved him. My son made it his mission to befriend and help educate the kid. By the end of the season, the kid and my son were friends, and you would have never known the season started with hate, blood, and tears.

I've found that being open and honest with kids is one of the best ways for them to see you as real. When I am not having the best day, I have no problem telling my kids,

"Mommy is not having a good day, and I know it's probably because I was rushing this morning and didn't pray." When my dad was going through a terminal illness, my kids saw me dealing with it all. They saw me going back and forth to the hospital to help take care of my dad. They saw me getting up early and staying up late praying for him. They even saw me crying, dealing with my emotions, and wiping my tears, telling them with much faith that God is a healer, and we were believing God for Papa's healing.

When my dad passed, in their confusion and hurt, they heard me declaring and proclaiming the same faith: that God is still good, still a healer, and still faithful. My children saw and heard me thanking God for the life my dad had, and the time God gave me with him. They saw me praise God for my dad's transition into the heavenly place he prayed and lived to be (with Jesus). They witnessed my faith in action. Through the tears, they saw my praise. If they follow any example, I pray they follow that one. No matter what they go through or how any prayer may not unfold as they hoped, I wish for them to hold on to who God is and believe that He is still good.

Chapter Seven
WHOLE & HOLY

———◈◈———

"May God himself, the God who makes everything
holy and whole, make you holy and whole, put
you together — spirit, soul, and body — and
keep you fit for the coming of our Master, Jesus
Christ. The One who called you is completely
dependable. If he said it, he'll do it."

—1 THESSALONIANS 5:23-24, MSG

As Christians, we spend so much time focusing on the spiritual upbringing of our children that we often overlook other elements God considers when He calls us to be whole. We teach our children many things to prepare them to become the best versions of themselves. Most parents genuinely desire not only what's best for their children but also want them to go farther than they have and to be better than they are. I believe God wants us to impart a full understanding of the importance of being whole in every way to our children.

Being whole refers to a state of completeness where an individual feels a sense of integration, harmony, and self-acceptance across various aspects of their life and identity. Wholeness implies that a person's well-being is balanced in every way. Well-being encompasses a holistic state of overall health, happiness, and contentment in different areas of life. It goes beyond physical health and includes a combination of physical, mental, emotional, spiritual, wealth, wisdom, knowledge, environment, and social well-being. When we live in wholeness, we experience the abundant life God desires for each of us. I am sure many may not agree with me, but the scripture doesn't lie. When the word of God says, "May God himself, the God who makes everything holy and whole, make you holy and whole, put you together – spirit, soul, and body," it doesn't only say soul or only say spirit. After stating "whole," it specifies "spirit, soul, and body."

Many adult Christians go through life feeling unhappy and incomplete. They love God and serve Him as often as possible, but something feels missing. They've been taught to focus on their spiritual walk and live holy lives, yet no one has provided them with insight into what happens after building a solid foundation. In fact, few churches offer support for growth beyond spiritual development. What about financial growth, social growth, professional growth, and emotional growth?

The church should also offer and impart these things. God's word in 3 John 1:2, ESV says, "I pray that all may go well with you and that you may be in good health, as it goes well with your soul." God desires more than just spiritual health for His people, and we should ensure our children know this and understand what it looks like in their lives.

Many adults who walk this earth were raised to focus on their financial well-being. They were taught that their financial stability and security were the most important parts of success and life. Parents taught these individuals how to manage finances responsibly, live within their means, generate income through multiple streams, and plan for the future. While all of this is great, it's not enough to feel whole. If it were enough, there wouldn't be so many miserable millionaires. One needs more than good finances to live a complete and abundant life.

Your mind encompasses several parts, all of which are important. Mental well-being involves the state of your mind and includes aspects like cognitive function, emotional regulation, and the ability to handle stress, anxiety, and other mental health challenges. Emotional well-being refers to your ability to understand, express, and manage your emotions effectively and involves having a healthy emotional balance as well as resilience in the face of life's challenges. This aspect of well-being relates to the health of your body, including factors such as nutrition, exercise, sleep, and managing illness or physical conditions.

Social well-being pertains to your relationships and so-cial interactions, involving a supportive social network, healthy relationships, and a sense of belonging and con-nectedness. This aspect of well-being is tied to your work or occupation and includes job satisfaction, a sense of purpose in your work, and a healthy work-life balance. Environmental well-being concerns your relationship with your physical surroundings and the natural envi-ronment, including living in a safe and clean space and practicing sustainability. Community well-being extends beyond personal relationships to the well-being of the communities and societies in which you live, including contributing to the betterment of your community and fostering social cohesion. Safety and security encompass feeling safe and secure in your physical environment and personal relationships, which is a fundamental as-pect of well-being that includes physical safety as well as emotional and psychological security. All of these are important aspects of being whole.

Oh, how amazing it would be if our children focused on God and allowed Him to make them whole in all aspects of their lives. We should help our children understand that they can be spiritually complete and still feel incomplete because they aren't living in the abundance and wholeness of God. The word says that God wants us whole in mind, body, and soul. This alone highlights how God desires our bodies to be healthy, our minds and mental well-being to be whole, and He definitely wants our souls to be whole, as

His word specifically states He wants our souls to prosper. God doesn't want us living in lack—in any area of life. We are living a lie if we think that God gets glory from us living in poverty. That is not of God. Jesus gave up riches in heaven to come to earth and live poor so we wouldn't have to. Look that up in the word at 2 Corinthians 8:9!

Contentment plays an important role in our feelings of wholeness. Scripture says to "Seek ye first the kingdom of heaven and all these other things shall be added." I believe that God wants to be first, but that doesn't mean He doesn't want us to seek out other things as well. Our children should know that it is okay to have dreams and goals. They should seek to better themselves, whether that includes going to college for knowledge, therapy for emotional and mental health improvements and management, or gaining financial literacy to plan for financial success. These things can't replace God and shouldn't come before our relationship with Christ, but they are important, and our children should understand this.

I believe parents should expose their children to each of these areas of well-being. Exposure brings possibilities. When kids are exposed to more, they perceive this exposure as a possibility and something that is indeed attainable. Exposing kids to possibilities, no matter where you are personally, is essential.

Holiness is still right. We can't become so fixated on seeking to be "whole" that we think we can live unholy. It is impossible. Holiness is synonymous with wholeness.

You can't be whole if you aren't holy; there will be a missing piece. Submitting to the Holy Spirit daily allows us to avoid being incomplete. The Holy Spirit leads and guides us. Obedience will direct us to seek the very things our body, mind, and soul need to be complete and whole.

Sustainability is what holiness brings into our lives. By living a holy life, we can maintain our wholeness. The Holy Spirit is a keeper, preserving our sense of completeness. When we step outside the bounds of holiness, we risk losing the blessings God has bestowed upon us. Peace is often the first thing to vanish. Without peace, we lose our sense of contentment. In the absence of contentment, we may begin to seek other things that deprive us in various areas. The balance in every aspect of our well-being disappears. When this occurs, we must return to our Father, God, to repent and regain our holiness so we can be restored to wholeness.

Understand that holiness has nothing to do with wearing long skirts, avoiding makeup or jewelry, never going anywhere other than church, or screaming and speaking in tongues. Holiness involves doing what you can to refrain from living a sinful life. To be holy means living a life that is set apart from that of the world and is intended to bring glory to God by obeying His word. There are no specific clothes or rituals that make anyone holy. Holiness fundamentally connects to having a relationship with God so that you can know what pleases Him and what will bring Him glory. Being holy should be regarded as something a person believes is attainable. The misconceptions surrounding "holiness" that have been imposed on people have had such a detrimental effect that many completely shy away from even trying. Those misconceptions are all religious and created by miserable, self-righteous individuals. We can teach our children what holiness is and how they can live a holy and whole life.

Chapter Eight
LET'S TALK, OUR FATHER

"Don't worry about anything; instead, pray about everything. Tell God what you need and thank him for all he has done. Then you will experience God's peace, which exceeds anything we can understand. His peace will guard your hearts and minds as you live in Christ Jesus."

—PHILIPPIANS 4:6-7, NLT

A life of prayer is something we all desperately need. There are great benefits for a person who prays and understands the importance of prayer. Prayer is simply our communication with God. Talking to God always brings me peace and reassurance that He is working on my behalf and that everything is going to be okay. Prayer allows me not only to give God my problems and concerns but also to ask for things for my family, friends, community, government, leaders, and so on. I know that using the word "etcetera" is often viewed as a cop-out, but in this case, it isn't. There is absolutely nothing we can't bring to God in prayer, and listing everything would be extreme and excessive, putting limits on what we can pray about. Because, quite frankly, I would leave too many things out in an attempt to list every issue or request for prayer. My experiences and knowledge are limited, but God is all-knowing, and nothing catches Him by surprise.

Here's something that shouldn't surprise you: you, as a parent, need a prayer life. The reality is that it is extremely hard to teach something to your children that you do not possess yourself. Having your own prayer life is likely more important than teaching your children to have one. A foundation of prayer is essential and cannot be omitted when raising children before the Lord.

Since childhood, I've been a person who prays. It came naturally. Praying wasn't something I thought about; I just knew that when challenges arose, God was my answer. This wasn't necessarily something taught to me in words or lessons; I picked up on it. For as long as I can remember, my parents were always praying. My mom would be in the kitchen cooking alone, but I would hear her talking. She wasn't on the phone; she was in deep prayer with God while performing everyday tasks like cooking. If my sisters and I got hurt, she would immediately begin to pray. Every day, I saw my dad either lying across his bed or sitting at the kitchen table with his Bible and notepad. He would read the word of God, study the word of God, and pray the word of God daily. My parents held full conversations with God in such a way that I naturally picked up on it and started talking to God myself.

I can't say that I prayed as much as they did when I was a child. In fact, the most consistent prayer my sisters and I shared as children was our nightly prayer right before bed. We all know it, the Lord's Prayer:

> *"Our Father who art in heaven, Hallowed be thy Name. Thy kingdom come. Thy will be done, on earth as it is in heaven. Give us this day our daily bread. And forgive us our trespasses, as we forgive those who trespass against us. And lead us not into temptation but deliver us from evil. For thine is the kingdom, and the power, and the glory, for ever and ever. Amen."*

What I do know is that when things came up, I would be on my knees praying, whether it was time for bed or not, and it wouldn't be the Lord's prayer. Living in Florida, I remember I had to be about eight years old when one of those dangerous hurricanes was heading in our direction. It sounded so scary outside. The electricity was out. The whole family sat on the couch as we listened to the winds roar and raindrops clash against the windows. I couldn't take it anymore and crawled under the coffee table in the middle of the living room. While on my knees, I buried my face into the carpet and began to pray that God would not only protect us but would calm the storm. I prayed with so much faith. Before I could even realize it, an alert came across the radio that the hurricane was shifting. It was at that point that I knew the power of prayer.

As I got older and experienced more, the more I prayed, and the more personal those prayers became. Through growth, I developed a better understanding of what prayer was and what it could do for me. Prayer is simply talking to God. It is truly just having a conversation and communicating with Him. As a child and teen, I was quite a talker. I pause and shake my head even as I type that because my children talk so much and seem never to stop, and my family loves to remind me that I used to talk just as much. Ah-ha. Nevertheless, talking to the One who knows me better than anyone and understands all my quirks became easier every day. Knowing and learning who God was and how amazing He truly is caused me to maintain a heart of worship in adoration of Him. In my youth, I learned that prayer really wasn't this hard concept that many tried to make it out to be. Prayer and worship literally saved my life in so many situations.

By the time I became pregnant with my first child, my son, prayer was something I couldn't live without. I understood the importance of prayer, and God placed it on my heart to instill a life of prayer and worship in my children. From the moment I knew my children were in my womb, I prayed over them out loud. I involved them in my devotion and meditation, speaking with them about God as if they were alive and breathing outside of me. I listened to worship music for hours and prayed out loud so that they could hear. This may sound crazy, but I was creating an atmosphere for my children.

Whether you know it or not, by the second trimester of pregnancy (around 18-24 weeks), a baby's ears have developed enough to perceive sounds from the outside world. They are particularly attuned to the sounds of their mother's body, such as her heartbeat and digestive noises. They can also hear sounds coming from outside the womb, including voices, music, and other environmental noises. Research suggests that babies can recognize and even prefer the sound of their mother's voice at birth. They grow familiar with the rhythm and intonation of their mother's speech patterns during pregnancy. Therefore, I was committed to ensuring that what they heard was the sound of worship, praise, and prayer.

I have only had two children, but I believe God allowed me to learn about each pregnancy very early on so that I could be intentional about setting an atmosphere of prayer and worship for them early. With my son, now ten years old, I found out I was pregnant at four weeks. I was only two days late and didn't even buy a test. I went straight to our family's clinic, and sure enough, the doctor confirmed I was indeed pregnant. I found out about my little Miss Sunshine, now approaching the big five years old, at five weeks pregnant. I actually knew I was carrying her the week prior to finding out, but decided not to test because it was the week of my son's big fifth birthday, and I didn't want to take the focus away from him.

Now, with my first, I was an unemployed attorney, and I was really trying to understand what exactly God's purpose was for my life. So, in this search, I naturally read my word, prayed, and listened to uplifting music. God placed it in my spirit that I should include my son in this time I spent with God. I didn't fully understand the effect of what I was doing throughout the pregnancy as a first-time mom, but I read enough to know that the unborn baby could somewhat hear what was happening outside of the womb and that the life inside of me could feel my emotions and mood. My Bible reading became reading to him as though he were three years old and wanted to hear a bedtime story. I prayed aloud and included him in my prayers by using words such as "us" and "we." When I wasn't in worship, I put headphones on my stomach and played worship music as well as Beethoven music. It was such an unexplainable calming experience. After seeing the effects of this with my first, I made it a duty to do it for my second as well.

Once my children were born, I prayed real prayers with them throughout the day. When they had their fussy moments with Daddy, my husband would play worship music, and I would pray. This was our thing. It may seem crazy, but I believe in including God in everything and allowing Him to relieve me of unnecessary stress. Our babies didn't have many fussy moments, and the ones they did have didn't last long because we put on "their" song. They both had that one song they loved, and we made it their go-to song for bedtime routines and any moment they needed to calm down. My son's song was Tye Tribbett's "What Can I Do." He would go completely silent as soon as he heard the intro of that song. Those lyrics resonated with my son. He lives by those lyrics, even at his tender age. My daughter's song was Darrel Walls' "I Will Exalt You." To this day, she has such a pure and bold adoration for God. I love to see her randomly worshipping. While we are a family that loves music and allows music to minister to us, we cherish prayer just as much.

As a mom, I truly wish I could protect my kids from all hurt, pain, and disappointment, and be with them every minute of the day to keep them safe and happy. I'm sure all loving parents feel this way. We don't want our children to endure anything other than happiness and goodness. If we could control it, they would never have to suffer or experience any emotion other than joy. But the reality is, we just can't. We can only control so much. However, I am a strong believer that God is the one who can be with them every moment of the day and protect them when I can't. This is why prayer, and a life of prayer, is so important to me. What mommy and daddy can't do, our heavenly Father can!

Teach your children not only that prayer is important but also how to pray. When the disciples went to Jesus and asked him to teach them to pray, He guided them with specific instructions. One of the most important things to remember about prayer is to be natural. In Matthew chapter six, Jesus helps us understand how to pray in a manner that God can hear us. He told his disciples that when we come to God, we shouldn't turn that into a stagy or dramatic production. It can confuse children when all the prayers they hear or see seem excessive and complicated. I love how Jesus instructs us and helps us understand how we should approach prayer.

Matthew 6:5-8, MSG says, *"And when you come before God, don't turn that into a theatrical production either. All these people making a regular show out of their prayers, hoping for fifteen minutes of fame! Do you think God sits in a box seat? Here's what I want you to do: Find a quiet, secluded place so you won't be tempted to role-play before God. Just be there as simply and honestly as you can manage. The focus will shift from you to God, and you will begin to sense his grace. The world is full of so-called prayer warriors who are prayer-ignorant. They're full of formulas and programs and advice, peddling techniques for getting what you want from God. Don't fall for that nonsense. This is your Father you are dealing with, and he knows better than you what you need. With a God like this loving you, you can pray very simply."*

He recited the same prayer my sisters and I said every night before bed, which we know as the Lord's Prayer. This is a prayer that many children recite each night before climbing into bed, often without understanding its meaning. However, the Lord's Prayer serves as an excellent starting point for teaching a child, or anyone, for that matter, how to pray. It simply cannot be the end. An explanation of the prayer should be provided, as there is more to it than just reciting the words. The prayer is intended as a guide and a format for how we pray. Then, prayers will become more personal and effective.

Teaching a child to pray effectively involves both guidance and allowing them to develop their own personal connection with God and their faith. You may not know where to begin teaching your child to pray, so I want to take a moment to share some tips. It starts with setting an example. You can't teach what you don't do yourself. As parents, we should model prayer by incorporating it into their daily routine. When children see their parents engaging in prayer, they are more likely to develop an interest and understanding of its importance. Parents should also explain the purpose of prayer to their children. Be open and talk to your child about prayer and its purpose. Explain that prayer is a way to communicate with God, express gratitude, seek guidance when uncertain, and find relief and peace. Keep prayer simple. Jesus told us in Matthew 6:6 that when we come to God in prayer, we should come as simply and honestly as we can manage. The younger they are, the more children may struggle to grasp complex spiritual concepts, so it's essential to keep prayers simple and relatable to their age. Encourage your children to speak from the heart and express their thoughts and feelings naturally when they talk to God. Teach your children basic prayers. Start by teaching your child basic prayers that are commonly used, such as the Lord's Prayer. Help them understand the meaning behind the words and encourage them to reflect on their significance. Help your children nurture a personal connection. Encourage your child to develop their relationship with their spiritual beliefs and God. Teach them that prayer is not just reciting words but also an opportunity to speak openly and honestly with God. Encourage them to share their joys, concerns, hopes, and dreams during their prayers, not just to ask God for things. Show them how to make prayer sacred by removing distractions. Dinner time is family time. When dinner is done cooking, everyone comes to the table, and we pray together. The television is turned off or muted, no phones are allowed at the table, and we take turns praying, all before we touch our plates or discuss our days with one another.

Chapter Nine
EXERCISE CONTROL & UNDERSTAND THE ASSIGNMENT

"He must manage his own family well, having children who respect and obey him."

—1 TIMOTHY 3:4, NLT

Order, control, structure, and discipline are all words that society has made to seem harsh and damaging to individuals. There is a negative connotation associated with authority, rules, and obedience. It is truly a trick of the enemy to shift the mindset of people away from the things of God and His ways. Every parent desires what is best for their child, but human ideas of what is best cannot compare to God's best. Living according to the will of God is what is best for us. God's way is the best; the more we align our lives with it, the better things will be for us and our families. I tell people all the time that partial obedience is still disobedience. Mistaken in our approach, we often practice some parts of God's word while feeling that others don't apply to us or are outdated. But God's word doesn't change; it is the same yesterday, today, and forever. Nevertheless, society has led the people of God to shy away from following God's way, especially in our parenting.

We must stop allowing the enemy to lie to us and fool us into believing that we can't control our children. It is our duty as parents to safeguard our children from things that are not good for them or that could initiate harmful consequences mentally, physically, emotionally, or spiritually. The pastor of the church I attend once preached a sermon where he discussed the importance of protecting what we allow to enter our bodies, consciousness, and minds through open gateways. Our gateways are essentially our five senses: smell, taste, hearing, sight, and touch. Parents should take an active role in guarding their children's gateways because, in their innocence and ignorance, they do not understand what certain things can lead to. In this way, we control and decide where we allow our children to go, what they watch and entertain on television or phones, what they listen to, and their environment. It may seem small, but it can have a huge effect.

My dad was quite strict when I was younger. There was a balance because my mom was easygoing, and we were aware of this. Eventually, my dad did lighten up as

I matured and grew older. But as a kid, I thought he was unreasonably strict. I remember always asking to spend the night with friends or family members, and he would not even consider the idea. In my youth, I didn't understand why. However, when I was in high school and college, I started learning about the sexual assaults experienced by people close to me, whether in their own homes or the homes of others. I took breaths of relief that my dad stood his ground in controlling our environment. These situations occurred in the very homes I would beg to sleep over at. My dad's wisdom and unwavering control over what he refused to allow to happen to me protected me from being exposed to such a traumatic experience.

At a certain age, it becomes harder to control your children, and you must lean on your influence rather than control. As children grow older, they gain a level of independence, making it easier for them to choose to open their own gateways. When this happens, parents cannot be blamed. As a kid, I wasn't allowed to listen to "secular" music. I use that term as my parents and religious leaders traditionally defined it for storytelling purposes. Music was considered secular if it wasn't about God and couldn't be sung in church. If the music was secular, we couldn't— and shouldn't—listen to it, according to Perry Cooper, Jr., my dad. By the time I reached middle school, I wanted to be more like the other kids and keep up with the current trends. If I heard my peers discussing certain music or artists, I would go home and search online on the fairly new internet. I opened my own gateways to the original "baddest" chick and learned every single one of her songs, lyric for lyric. Those lyrics ran through my young mind and sparked a fascination with being the "baddest" and desiring to do what the "baddest" rapped about. Something as simple as music has a huge impact on us. The things we listen to enter our minds and can take root, potentially becoming a problem in the future. Music can alter a person's entire mood. Someone who listens to sad, depressing music is likely to experience depression or unexplained sadness. So as a parent with personal understanding, I not only monitor what my children listen to, but I also explain to them why they cannot listen to it. I don't think I am as extreme as my dad was, who only allowed gospel/Jesus music. However, there is a rule that my husband or I must listen to any new artist they want to explore before it can be added to their library.

At an early age, show and explain to your children that you expect them to give their best and that you won't accept anything less. Ensure it is clear that, no matter what, nothing will change your love for them. Just as in our adult relationships (employment, friendships, etc.), we make our expectations known and clear; we should do the same for our children.

Again, it is important to remember that kids mimic those who influence them. Thus, it is learned behavior that sticks with children. We know this to be true because many of us are trying to unlearn the traumatic and toxic behaviors we picked up as children from our parents or adults we spent a lot of time with. This is why I strive to be the parent I needed and wanted as a child, so that I can break some of these generational curses.

Be clear: if children exhibit behaviors that don't reflect what you are teaching, they are likely receiving those messages through one of their gateways. It may not necessarily come from you; it could be from television, social media, or other children. However, as parents, we have the responsibility to address and correct these behaviors immediately. We have a duty to be intentional in our assignment given by God. Allowing your children to act without consequences does not reflect God's will. Yes, this is where I discuss discipline. No one wants to talk about discipline anymore, yet these undisciplined children are growing into adults who lack a sense of authority, rules, and societal order.

It is time for us to make a conscious decision to change our mindset and how we view discipline. Discipline isn't just about punishing children. Discipline is the practice of training individuals to obey rules or a code of behavior, utilizing punishment to correct disobedience. Teaching children to be orderly, self-controlled, and respectful will equip them with the tools to thrive in a world where they are expected to abide by laws, respect others, and succeed in life. Whether you realize it or not, you teach your children discipline when you ensure they do homework, encourage good hygiene and exercise, inspire Bible reading, prayer, and attending church, and promote healthy eating habits. Without these practices, we set them up for unnecessary struggles. Most children who lack parents promoting these simple habits are essentially raising themselves, seeking guidance from outside influences such as their community, television, and peers. I've heard people argue that discipline instills fear, asserting that once a person no longer fears the consequences, they will engage in the very behaviors they were instructed to avoid. Interestingly, laws create a certain level of fear to deter people from breaking them. What is the difference? Let's also remember that true love casts out fear. Thus, a child who is loved by a parent does not fear the parent but rather the consequence. I see no issue with acknowledging the fear of consequences. God said the wages of sin are death, meaning that the consequence of living a sinful life is death. I prefer not to face that consequence.

Consistency plays a crucial role in maintaining order and structure at home. Inconsistency in discipline will not help a child respect you; in fact, it has the opposite effect. A consistent and predictable home environment helps children understand rules, expectations, and consequences. Inconsistent parenting can lead to confusion and insecurity, which may manifest in behavioral issues. Be committed to following through with promised consequences for misbehavior. Structure provides a framework for setting and enforcing boundaries and rules. Children need clear guidelines to comprehend what is expected of them and what behaviors are acceptable. Consistent enforcement of rules helps children develop a sense of responsibility and accountability. They thrive when they know what to expect. Establishing routines and structures in their daily lives creates a sense of consistency and predictability. This helps children feel secure and reduces anxiety, as they can antici-pate what will happen next. I maintain a daily schedule for my children. They know precisely what to do from the time they get out of school until they go to bed. Time is allocated for reading and homework, sports and activities, screen time, family dinner, baths, and bedtime. Structured rou-tines assist children in learning time management skills. They gain an understanding of how to allocate their time for various activities, including schoolwork, chores, and leisure. This prepares them for future responsibilities and commitments while maintaining balance. Who wouldn't want to help their children acquire these life skills by the time they leave the nest?

There is always the idea of being too strict or overly controlling, which can have a negative effect, causing chil-dren to rebel. There are numerous parenting methods and ideas about the best way to raise kids. My thoughts are to simply be to our children as our heavenly Father is to us. God, our Father, gives us instructions and sets expecta-tions through His word; when we go against that, there are consequences. He still loves us, provides our needs, and gives grace and mercy, allowing us to correct our behav-iors for better outcomes. God's expectations of His children are clear. Likewise, parents should have clear expectations for their children. My children know that I do not expect perfection from them, but I do expect their best in education, how they treat others, and anything they set out to accomplish. We should not support or accept behaviors or actions from our children that contradict God's word. It is indeed possible to disapprove of certain behaviors while still loving them unconditionally. Accepting and supporting actions that go against God's word, without attempting to correct or guide them towards God's way, leads us to compromise.

As long as children are under your care and control, you must exercise the authority that God has entrusted you with. Raising children in the right way is an assignment and part of the purpose that God has for your life. Everything after that is up to God. I believe we should strive to fulfill all our Godly assignments well and remain faithful to them. God gave you children to help them become what He intended for them to be, and that journey begins when they are young. You can't wait until your children are 16 or 17 years old to start trying to enforce rules and control their every move. This must be established from the very beginning, at an early age. When children understand your role, respect your authority, and trust your judgment, obeying you will come more easily as they grow older. If your children are teens and you want to adopt a more Godly parenting approach, you should be open and honest with your teenagers and clearly communicate that things will be changing and explain why. You will need to have patience during this parenting transition, but I believe God will support you through the remaining years.

Emotionally healthy children are often raised in homes that provide order and structure. Ask teachers and principals how likely it is for them to have students whose active and present parents misbehave in school. I believe that order and structure can help children regulate their emotions. Routines can serve as anchor points during stressful times or transitions, helping children maintain a sense of stability and emotional well-being. I recall when my baby girl was around 20 months old; she started having tantrums. These tantrums seemed to come out of nowhere, but I knew this behavior originated from daycare. I consistently got to her level and told her that I didn't accept her attitude or behavior. I prayed for her. At night, I would anoint her and pray over her with conviction. I would let her hear me tell God that I needed patience, but I wouldn't accept what was happening because that was not my child. I remained consistent and never allowed her to have her way. Before her second birthday, that tantrum phase was over. She returned to being the lovable little girl I knew. The enemy's job is to wear the saints out, and he will use anyone, especially our children, to do that. I refused to accept this because I know the will of God for my life and my children's lives. She learned early on that her mother won't just allow her to be like everyone else and accept the terrible twos behavior. The things we choose to accept enable the behavior, and we must then deal with the consequences as it continues and worsens. If I had ignored the tantrums and simply accepted that this was just a phase that all two-year-olds go through, I believe that behavior would have worsened and could have sown a seed of entitlement, anger issues, or more.

A home of peace always reflects a sense of order and structure. God is the Prince of Peace, and He doesn't dwell in confusion or chaos. Order within the home establishes a strong familial foundation. Orderliness is a characteristic of all of God's works. If your home feels like a circus and lacks real structure, it is not too late to reset and ask God to guide you in bringing order to your home. You will need to help your children understand that setting rules, boundaries, and expectations is essential for being the parent they need at this stage of their lives. For true peace, start with prayer. Sorry y'all, but sage will not suffice. I pray for a peaceful home every day, and have had people tell me they feel a sense of peace there and get the best rest at my home. It's truly God's peace and the atmosphere I am intentionally creating for my family.

Chapter Ten

THE ULTIMATE CLASSROOM

---

*"For I have chosen him, so that he will direct his children
and his household after him to keep the way of the Lord
by doing what is right and just, so that the Lord will
bring about for Abraham what he has promised him."*

—GENESIS 18:19, NIV

Contrary to what most people want to believe, the school is NOT responsible for raising your children, babysitting your children, or teaching them everything they will ever need to know. That is the parents' responsibility. As we can see now, the government can decide what schools teach and do not teach. Learning, knowledge, and wisdom should all start at home. Home is your child's first classroom. Love and hate are taught at home. All our morals and beliefs originate from where and how we were raised.

Teachers and schools will change, but the home will remain the real classroom. The things that are taught at home will go farther than anything that is taught in a school. A home that relies on the word of God as the main curriculum is a home setting their family up to flourish. Incorporating the scriptures in our homes by not just reading but living out the word demonstrates what God's word means and how to apply scripture to everyday life.

It is best to teach our children to move beyond tradition and ritual when creating a foundation with Christ. While some traditions may bring us closer to God, they should be explored and explained to transcend mere ritual. It is essential to critically examine our traditions, seeking to align them with the core teachings of Christianity as well as our personal relationship with God. Doing so will provide a stronger foundation for our children to follow.

Now I know and understand two things. One is that we all have different circumstances and barriers that have a direct effect on how we parent and the time we can invest in personally teaching our children. The other is that every child is different, so what works for one may not work for another. In any situation, I know that God understands all of this and can and will provide you with everything you need to be your child's leading teacher in their youth. One of my daily prayers is asking God to give me everything I need to fulfill my responsibilities; grant me wisdom, knowledge, patience, grace, and strength for whatever is at hand on that day. Every day involves being a mother and my children's main teacher.

School should not be the place where everything is introduced to your child. Children who have no foundational understanding of a concept tend to be harder to teach. Ask a kindergarten teacher who has a class where some of the students do not know their numbers or letters. Those who know the ABC song but don't recognize the letters when shown have a disadvantage compared to those who come in knowing some of the letters. I empathize with teachers trying to introduce and teach letters to children in a classroom setting at this stage, when they have little to no understanding of letter recognition. It is difficult for these teachers. Not only is it hard for the teacher, but those children can become problematic out of the frustration of feeling like they can't learn. The truth is, they are at a disadvantage because they should have been introduced to and taught some of the concepts prior to starting school. The curriculum isn't designed to start from ground zero. I've prided myself on ensuring I teach my children things before they are brought up in school, so that when they are in the classroom, they are gaining a better understanding of the concept and can follow along with the teacher to refine the skills and knowledge they do have. And Lord forbid the curriculum doesn't include an important concept they will need in the future, or just good knowledge to have; at least they won't be ignorant of the concept because I have taught them first at home.

This applies to every aspect of their lives. Home is the classroom of life, not just a place for intelligence. Children learn to love at home. They first learn to handle conflict in the home, whether by resolving issues with siblings or observing their parents in conflict. The truth is, if the home is the first classroom, that means you are the first teacher. You teach and show your babies and toddlers how to manage their emotions and feelings. You teach them how to prioritize people and things. You guide them in loving God and in leaning on Him in every situation or season.

The best part about your home being the ultimate classroom for your children is that you can control what the curriculum will be. You have the authority to decide what is taught and what isn't. Use this power to cultivate children who love God, love people, love themselves, and desire a life that is pleasing to God. Reflect on your childhood and the lessons you absorbed from your home. Many things you learned simply by observing them being done repeatedly. Not that your parents were intentionally trying to teach you, but you picked them up because they were happening in the classroom at home. The home in which our children are raised should be the training ground for everything. If done correctly, the important lessons taught will shape your children, and they will retain those lessons, making them their own.

Adults tend to make things more difficult than they need to be. Teachable moments are all around us, and they don't have to be forced. A toddler can bring a toy block to you, and you can simply say, "What color is this?" Then you have a short period of teaching colors. They may not get them all right, but they are indeed learning their colors while playing with blocks. The same applies to teaching children about God. You don't have to force God down your children's throats night and day. Talking about God in a regular, non-forceful way does much more than sitting down for a full-blown Bible study or lesson. Just make God a part of the family. I love pointing out what God is doing or has done. "Wow. God surely worked that out for you." "I'm so glad that God is our healer." Talk about God in relevant situations for your children as opportunities arise, as often as possible. Use these times as teaching moments and show them how God shows up in everything concerning them. This teaches them who God is to and for them. Just as you talk about grandma and grandpa or the dog, talk about God and watch how connected they get with Him. They will know Him as a very "present" help.

Remember, your classroom is where you create the environment. God will dwell where He is welcomed. Let your children hear you speak about your need for God and the adoration you have for Him. Children cling to what makes them feel safe. Teach them to find safety in God. They will typically take your lead. I know that for my kids, their first observation of how I interact with someone usually determines whether they trust that person or feel comfortable with them. I try to be very mindful of this because nonverbal communication is, by far, the loudest and most honest.

Body language and facial expressions teach your children whom you like and dislike. It also teaches them how to treat people they do and don't like. If I throw my hands up with a smile on my face, my children will immediately get excited and ask what happened. They've learned over time that this particular nonverbal reaction must mean I am giving thanks to God for something.

There are several ways a teacher can assess whether a student is fully understanding and learning what is being taught. A teacher can only explain and work out examples on the board so many times before it is necessary to call a student up to work it out on their own to see if they understand the concept. After allowing some group practice as a class, a teacher moves on to assignments, quizzes, and tests. Any good teacher will always tell their students that if they need help understanding, they should ask questions. To know if a person is learning, one must allow and encourage question asking. Asking questions shows an interest in knowing more and fully understanding. Encourage your children to ask questions about faith, spirituality, and God. I believe they should even be able to ask questions about our decisions and rules. Sometimes people rebel against things they don't understand. How will they understand if they can't ask questions that clarify any confusion they may have? Be open to their curiosity about God and provide thoughtful, age-appropriate answers. I like to give a scripture that will answer a question because this isn't something that I am making up, but comes right from the word of God. It's important for you to know that it is okay if you don't have all the answers to their questions. Please don't get mad or frustrated with your children or their inquisitiveness. It's a classroom, so now it is time to do a project by exploring the questions together. I promise this will leave a lasting impression on your child and can be a meaningful experience. Children see that their parents aren't perfect and don't know it all, which humanizes you in their eyes, making you more relatable.

I am not raising perfect children. I am raising individuals who love, honor, and revere God and want to please Him personally. Our goal shouldn't be to make our children think they should be perfect or never make mistakes. In fact, children need to see that we, as parents or adults, aren't perfect either. Let your home be a classroom with a teacher who apologizes when they are wrong and doesn't make excuses when they make a mistake. I'll be honest, when we have our daily car ride prayers, I am intentional about repenting. I want them to hear their mom go to God when I have fallen short and need His blood to cleanse me of my sins. It should be taught that sin is sin, no matter how we try to label it as minor or major. If I have been lazy or procrastinated, I let them hear me repent for that. When I have been snappy, moody, or impatient with them, I try to apologize and explain where the frustration is coming from. But I always ask God for forgiveness out loud so they can hear. They need to know we aren't just adults laying down the law, preaching, and teaching while not living a life that aligns with what we expect from them. Even more importantly, they need to know that they will still be loved by us and God when they make mistakes or don't obey our rules and expectations.

One day, my daughter was having an off day. At her young age, things just weren't going her way, so she was reacting like most self-absorbed individuals do when things aren't going their way. After I noticed that it was gradually getting worse and she wasn't calming down, I had to address it. I told her she wasn't being very nice and that I didn't like how she was acting. Later that day, she came to me and asked, "Mommy, does God still love me when I am not being nice?" This truly warmed my heart, and I knew it was the perfect teaching moment. With a smile, I responded, "Baby girl, God loves us when we aren't being nice; He loves us when we aren't being lovable; He loves us when we are in trouble. God loves us when we are doing great and when we are bad. There is absolutely nothing you can do to make God stop loving you!" She got so excited, and I know that lesson and knowledge of God's love for her stuck with her because now, over a year later, she still randomly proclaims, "God loves me so much!"

This is what it is all about: allowing your kids to know who God is. God is a loving God. God is a just God. God is our redeemer, and when we come to Him sincerely about our flaws and imperfections, He will spend time helping us overcome those imperfections. Help your children not to dwell too much on their imperfections, so much so that they miss the love and concern that God has for them. My son is very hard on himself when he makes mistakes. The mistakes can be in drawing, sports, video games, or academics. It isn't always behavioral or due to bad choices. He has a type A personality like his mother. But I often get concerned for him because not only is he a perfectionist, but he also dislikes disappointing others. He breaks down if he feels he has disappointed his parents, but mostly God. He is quick to confess and repents faster than I ever did at his age. This isn't out of fear but from a true sense of honor and reverence for his parents and God. So, after he is disciplined, we try to overload him with love and affirmations. Ensure that in your home, a God learning center, you always lead and end with the love of God.

As your child grows older, they may have questions or doubts about their faith. Encourage open conversations and provide resources for them to explore different perspectives. Help them understand that spiritual growth is a lifelong journey. Most importantly, be patient with them. Understand that your children may have their own unique paths, and it may take time for them to embrace and comprehend their faith fully. However, you can lay a strong foundation.

A strong foundation is a true testament to helping children create a bond with God, one that encourages them to intentionally and freely choose to stay with Him. These are qualities that merely attending church twice a week cannot instill. It requires more than church involvement to build a solid relationship with God. True understanding and experience with Him are essential for making one's heart love Him more than anything else. A child who loves God grows into an adult who loves God. A person who genuinely loves God will also love God's people.

Raising children to become loving, compassionate adults begins with teaching them these virtues while they are young. Teach your children the importance of loving and caring for others. Encourage acts of kindness and charity as expressions of their faith. Show them how to engage in ministry and serve outside of the church. A crucial aspect of the Christian faith involves evangelism and helping those in need, and our children must understand why this is important. In your home, teach them how blessed they are and how God has commissioned us to be His hands and feet to reach out to those in the world. After having my first child, I started making Blessing Bags. The bags included travel-sized hygiene products, nonperishable snacks, gift cards to fast food restaurants, sandwiches, socks, and sometimes cash. I would keep them in the car and offer them to the homeless people I encountered along the way. Other times, I would prepare meals and go to local parks or homeless sites to give them out. My then three-year-old son was always with me during these times, and he was excited to help me make the bags. My husband often gives money out of his pocket to random people without mentioning it. My kids would come home saying, "Dad gave a man at Walmart money" or "Dad paid for their food." Our children have witnessed us giving outside of the church walls to complete strangers, and they understand this practice well. So much so that they are now eager to give money to people on the side of the road. My son is particularly enthusiastic about this and never misses an opportunity to help. It doesn't matter if all he has is a twenty-dollar bill he just received as allowance; he doesn't hesitate to give it to someone in need. I love what he always says afterward: "God will bless me with more; I'm not worried." He doesn't ask for permission to give; he simply does it. The mother in me sometimes urges him to be cautious before approaching people or rolling down the window. I always feel a sense of accomplishment when I hear my children praying for those in need and thanking God for the blessings they do have. They don't just help by giving; they also send up prayers for these individuals. These are things that just can't be taught or experienced by merely going to church.

Attending church alone is not sufficient to establish a solid foundation for your children to grow up as Christians who truly love and understand God. Just going to church will not strengthen or build your own relationship with God. We have a duty to live out this life every day. Seeking God and His way daily is essential. Reading a scripture a day and genuinely meditating on it allows God's word to take root in your heart. To lead and teach your children, you must prepare and know the curriculum as well. Study God's word. Seek wisdom. It doesn't matter if you are a single mother or father, or a grandmother raising your grandchildren, or a legal guardian of children. We all have a responsibility to raise these children in the way of God. I believe that once we truly follow God's way, we will witness a tremendous change in our children and the adults they will become. This generation needs God. Let's lead them to Him. Let's demonstrate how to live for Him. Let's introduce them to understanding who He is so they can build their own relationship with Him. If done correctly, they won't ever want to leave God. While doing this for them, I challenge you to do it for yourself as well. Be renewed!

www.ingramcontent.com/pod-product-compliance
Lightning Source LLC
Chambersburg PA
CBHW060058150626
46556CB00017BA/1904